DATE DUE

American Lives

George Washington

Rick Burke

Heinemann Library
Chicago, Illinois

© 2003 Heinemann Library
a division of Reed Elsevier Inc.
Chicago, Illinois

Customer Service 888-454-2279

Visit our website at www.heinemannlibrary.com

Created by the publishing team
at Heinemann Library

Designed by Ginkgo Creative, Inc.
Photo Research by Kathryn Creech
Printed and Bound in the United States by
Lake Book Manufacturing, Inc.

07 06 05 04 03
10 9 8 7 6 5 4 3 2 1

Library of Congress Cataloging-in-Publication Data
Burke, Rick, 1957-
  George Washington / Rick Burke.
     p. cm. — (American lives)
Summary: A biography of George Washington,
Commander in Chief of the Continental Army and
first president of the United States.
Includes bibliographical references and index.
  ISBN 1-40340-158-6 ((lib. bdg.)) —
  ISBN 1-40340-414-3 ((pbk.))
  1. Washington, George, 1732-1799—Juvenile
literature. 2. Presidents—United States—
Biography—Juvenile literature. [1. Washington,
George, 1732-1799. 2. Presidents.] I. Title.
  E312.66 .B88 2002
  973.4'1'092—dc21
                                         2002004557

Acknowledgments
The author and publishers are grateful to the
following for permission to reproduce copyright
material: p. 4 Andrew W. Mellon Collection,
1947.17.16, National Gallery of Art, Washington,
D.C.; p. 5 Hisham F. Ibrahim/PhotoDisc; pp. 6, 8L,
13, 16 The Granger Collection, New York; pp. 7,
10, 11, 12, 18 North Wind Picture Archives; p. 8R
Mount Vernon Ladies' Association; p. 9 The
Library of Congress; p. 14 James P. Blair/Corbis; p.
15 Hulton Archive/Getty Images; p. 20 The Palma
Collection/PhotoDisc; p. 19 Bridgeman Art Library;
p. 22 Art Resource; pp. 23, 24, 25 Corbis; p. 26
Burstein Collection/Corbis; p. 27 Réunion des
Musées Nationaux/Art Resource; p. 28 National
Portrait Gallery, Smithsonian Institution/Art
Resource; p. 29 Jeremy Woodhouse/PhotoDisc

Cover photograph: Philadelphia Museum of Art/
Corbis

Special thanks to Patrick Halladay for his help in
the preparation of this book. Rick Burke thanks
Helen, the best mom any boy could ever have.

Every effort has been made to contact copyright
holders of any material reproduced in this book.
Any omissions will be rectified in subsequent
printings if notice is given to the publisher.

Some words are shown in bold, **like this.** You can
find out what they mean by looking in the glossary.

The image of George Washington on the cover of this book
was painted by Adolph Ulrich Wertmuller in 1794.

Contents

Leader of a Nation

George Washington was the first president of the United States, but he was much more than that. Every time his country needed him, he did everything he could to help. The United States is strong and free today partly because of Washington and his brave actions.

Washington helped his country four times and always returned to his farm and his own life. He could have held onto power. He could have made people do exactly what he wanted. But he didn't think acting that way was right.

Because of all the things Washington did to help form the United States, he became known as "the father of his country."

The Washington Monument is a reminder of what Washington did for his country.

Washington had the power to make himself king of the United States, and some people thought he should do just that. But he thought that the people of the United States should be able to pick their own leader.

Washington helped make being president one of the most powerful positions in the world. He also helped shape his country. It became a place that people from around the world wanted to make their home.

Washington Firsts

- *First president of the United States.*
- *First president to declare Thanksgiving a national holiday.*
- *First president to appear on a postage stamp.*

Childhood

George Washington was born on February 22, 1732, in Westmoreland County, Virginia. George was the son of Augustine Washington and his second wife, Mary Ball. His family was very wealthy.

Augustine died when George was just eleven years old. If Augustine had lived, George would have gone to the best schools in England. **Tutors** taught George instead. George was good at math, but what he loved most was being outside and riding horses.

This painting shows George's mother, whose full name was Mary Ball Washington.

The Life of George Washington

1732	1755	1774	1775
Born on February 22 in Virginia.	*Fought for the British in the French and Indian War.*	*Served in First* **Continental** *Congress.*	*Became the leader of American forces in the* **Revolutionary War.**

This drawing is of George's brother Lawrence, who served in the British army. George wanted to be like him.

George tried to obey his mother, but he didn't always agree with her. George liked to make his own decisions.

George and his older brother Lawrence got to be good friends. When George was a teenager, Lawrence said he could get George into the British navy. George's mother wouldn't let him go. George told himself that someday he would be in charge of himself.

Washington's Birthday

Washington was born on February 11, 1732, under an old calendar. When the way of counting days and months changed, so did Washington's birthday. Because of the change, we celebrate Washington's birthday on February 22.

1781	1789	1792	1799
Won the war against the British.	*Elected first president of the United States.*	*Reelected president.*	*Died on December 14 at Mount Vernon.*

Surveyor

George found his father's **surveyor** tools in a barn and taught himself how to use them. George was good at surveying, and he made a lot of money doing it. Sometimes, he would buy land with the money he had made.

His job took him far away from home and gave him a chance to see different parts of the American **colonies.** George was given the job of surveying and mapping the lands owned by Lord Fairfax. Fairfax owned millions of **acres** of land in the colonies.

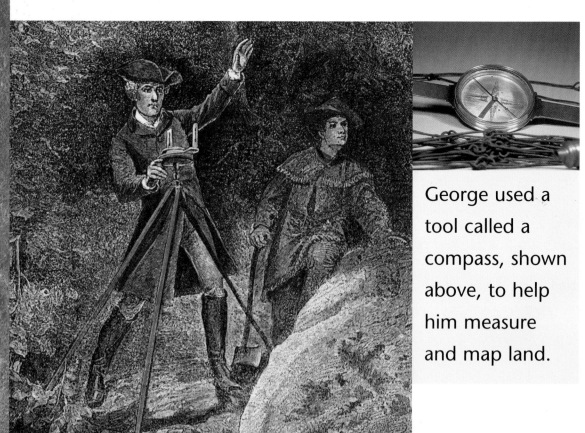

George used a tool called a compass, shown above, to help him measure and map land.

In 1747, George made this map of a field in which tulips were grown.

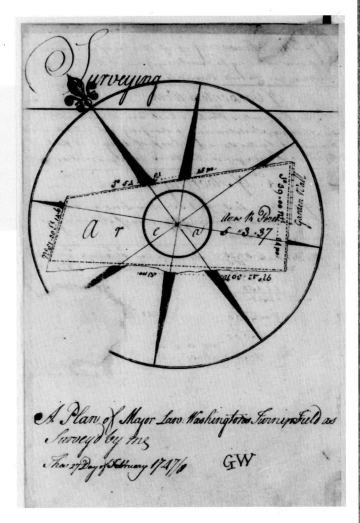

By the time he was 21 years old, George was more than 6 feet (1.8 meters) tall. Most of the men in the colonies were shorter. George was also very strong and a powerful wrestler.

When he wasn't surveying, George liked to spend time at his brother Lawrence's **plantation,** Mount Vernon. George loved to dance at Lawrence's parties. After Lawrence died in 1752, George lived at Mount Vernon. Later, when Lawrence's wife and daughter died, George became the owner of Mount Vernon.

French and Indian War

In 1754, both England and France wanted to own land in North America. They wanted the fur of the animals that lived there because the fur was worth lots of money. Both countries fought a war to decide who owned the land. It became known as the French and Indian War.

This picture shows what George probably looked like when he was 25. He fought for the British in the war.

George was a soldier in the **militia.** He was sent to try to get three Indian tribes to be on England's side during the war. One Indian tribe liked George so much that they made him a member of their tribe. They gave him the Indian name of *Conotocarious*.

Washington and Gist's mission was to deliver a message to French soldiers near the Ohio River.

One day George and Christopher Gist, another **surveyor,** were sent on a **mission.** They took an Indian guide with them. During the trip, the guide turned around and fired his gun at George, but he missed. The guide ran behind a tree to reload his gun, but George quickly wrestled it away from him.

Just as Gist was about to shoot the guide, George pulled Gist's gun away. He wouldn't allow someone without a weapon to be killed. George let the guide go.

Conotocarious

Conotocarious *means "devourer of villages."* *It was also the name given to Washington's grandfather when he fought battles with the Indian tribes.*

Martha and the War's End

George became a colonel in the British army. He helped General Edward Braddock, the leader of the army. On a march to a fort, the French army surprised the British army and attacked.

General Braddock was killed in the surprise attack, but the British won the French and Indian War.

Both George and Braddock were on the battlefield telling their soldiers how to fight. George had two horses shot and killed from under him. Four bullets passed through his coat. George left the army in 1759 and went back to Mount Vernon.

George met a young **widow** while he was in the army. Her name was Martha Dandridge Custis. Martha was one of the richest people in the **colonies.** She owned thousands of **acres** of land and hundreds of **slaves.**

John

When Martha's son John died, George and Martha adopted two of John's children.

George and Martha married on January 6, 1759. Martha had two children, John and Patsy, from her first marriage. George treated them like they were his own children. He now had a wife and his own family.

George and Martha were both 27 when they were married. They had only known each other for a few weeks.

Farmer

George moved Martha and the children to Mount Vernon. He wanted to make sure that the lands he and Martha owned made money. Most Virginia farmers in George Washington's time grew tobacco. The tobacco was sold in Europe, which made farmers rich. But growing only one kind of crop hurt the soil.

George grew wheat and other food products. He helped keep his soil rich by changing the crops he grew every few years. Washington also raised mules.

People can still visit Mount Vernon. The buildings look like they did in 1799, the last year George lived there.

George also designed and built a barn with sixteen sides instead of the normal four. His **slaves** could **thresh** wheat inside the large barn and out of the rain. This way, wheat didn't rot in the fields, and the slaves didn't get in each other's way.

Slaves worked at Mount Vernon. The slaves George owned were set free when George died.

For fun, George liked to go fox hunting. He and his friends would ride horses and chase a fox. George was an excellent rider, and not everyone could keep up with him.

Continental Congress

By the 1770s, the **colonists** of North America didn't like being told what to do by England, the country that ruled the colonies. Many colonists wanted to form their own country.

In 1774, George Washington was picked to be part of the **Continental Congress** in Philadelphia, Pennsylvania. The Congress decided that England could no longer make rules for the colonies.

The next year, during the Second Continental Congress, Washington offered to lead an army to fight the British. England still wanted to control the colonies. Every Congress member voted for George to be the leader of the army.

By the time Washington was elected to lead the army, the first battles of the **Revolutionary War** had been fought.

Many colonists did not want a war with England. They hoped England would let the colonists form their own country. Others believed there would be a war. They hoped France would help the colonists fight.

All the men in the Congress knew that they would be punished if England won the war. Washington tried to be brave. He knew that a war was coming and that it was his job to win that war. He also knew that it wouldn't be easy.

Thirteen Original Colonies

The areas labeled "Spanish Territory" and "Spanish Florida" were controlled by Spain.

Leader of the Army

The king of England sent thousands of soldiers to the **colonies** to try to beat Washington's army. Washington's army didn't have many men. The men Washington did have weren't soldiers. They had to be taught how to fight.

During the winter of 1775, Washington's army was camped in Massachusetts. A snowball fight started and turned into a **riot** that couldn't be stopped. Washington heard the riot and hopped on his horse. He raced across a field, grabbed two of the biggest men, and made them stop fighting. The riot stopped instantly because all of the men looked up to Washington.

Washington is shown taking command of the army in this picture.

This painting shows Washington and his men crossing the Delaware River on their way to victory in the Battle of Trenton.

The men in Washington's army loved him because he was a good leader. He taught his soldiers to fight for one united country, the United States, and not just for one colony. He knew how to beat the British army because he had studied how they fought during the French and Indian War.

Washington was as smart as the foxes he hunted at Mount Vernon. On a stormy Christmas night in 1776, he and his army crossed the Delaware River and beat the British army in a battle at Trenton, New Jersey.

The War Ends

Washington's army faced the biggest test of the war during the winter of 1777 to 1778 at Valley Forge, Pennsylvania. The army of 11,000 men spent a cold, icy winter without enough food, clothing, or warm places to sleep.

More than 2,500 men died that winter. Some men talked about going home or taking over the army. But the army stayed

Washington knew his soldiers at Valley Forge needed food and clothes.

together because the men knew Washington was just as cold and hungry as they were. They knew that he could help them beat the British.

The Americans began to win the war in February 1778. France decided to join the fight against the British. The French government sent their best general, thousands of soldiers, and many ships. Washington now had the army he needed to win the war.

In 1781, Washington trapped Lord Cornwallis and his British army at Yorktown, Virginia. The British gave up and sailed home. Washington and his army had won. Now, there could be no doubt that the United States of America was a free country.

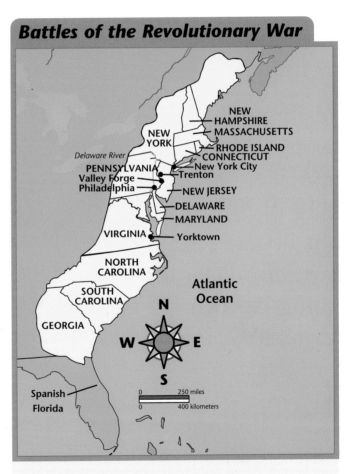

Battles of the Revolutionary War

NEW HAMPSHIRE
MASSACHUSETTS
NEW YORK
RHODE ISLAND
CONNECTICUT
Delaware River
New York City
PENNSYLVANIA
Valley Forge
Trenton
Philadelphia
NEW JERSEY
DELAWARE
MARYLAND
VIRGINIA
Yorktown
NORTH CAROLINA
Atlantic Ocean
SOUTH CAROLINA
GEORGIA

N
W   E
S

Spanish Florida

0   250 miles
0   400 kilometers

Some of the cities where battles took place are shown on the map above.

A New Nation

Washington quit his job as leader of the army on December 19, 1783. The men of his army and the rest of the country loved Washington for winning the war.

Washington could have used the army to make himself the king of America, but he didn't. He was happy about going back to Mount Vernon.

After the war, Washington planned on living the rest of his life at Mount Vernon.

Washington's Teeth

Washington wore false teeth when he was older. They were made from cow teeth, human teeth, and ivory from the tusks of elephants. They were not made of wood.

Washington was the first to sign the Constitution when it was finished.

In 1787, the United States needed Washington again. The state leaders weren't doing what was best for a united country. Instead, they wanted whatever was best for their own states. So they met in the city of Philadelphia, Pennsylvania, at the **Constitutional Convention.** George was asked to be in charge of the convention.

The leaders met to write a document of laws and rules, known as a constitution, to make the nation stronger. They decided that the country needed one man, a president, to lead the country. Everyone at the convention voted for Washington to be president.

President

When Washington rode to New York City, the first capital of the United States, people lined the roads cheering. They lit bonfires and shot cannons to show their love for him.

As president, Washington did many good things. Probably the best thing he did was to keep the young country out of wars. The United States was a new nation and it wasn't as strong as some European countries were. Staying out of wars made the country stronger and helped it to survive.

Washington rode to New York City in 1789. Large crowds gathered to welcome him in every town along the way.

This picture shows Washington with government leaders Henry Knox, Alexander Hamilton, Thomas Jefferson, and Edmund Randolph.

Washington had smart, talented people like Alexander Hamilton and Thomas Jefferson to give him advice about what was best for the nation. They did argue about some things. Hamilton thought the states should have less power and the nation should be friendly with England. Jefferson thought the states should have more power and be friendly with France.

Washington listened to both men and slowly made his own decisions. He had learned that lesson as a small boy when he realized that he didn't want his mother to make all his decisions.

Farewell

George Washington was elected to another four-year **term** in 1792. He soon made an agreement with the country of Spain that let the United States use the Mississippi River and the city of New Orleans.

Washington had learned how important rivers were for travel when he was a **surveyor.** He also knew the value of land. He had bought land west of the **colonies** when he was a young man. He knew that the country would continue to get bigger and that people would need more land.

The Growing Nation

Great Lakes

Missouri River

Ohio River

Mississippi River

U.S. Territory Gained by Treaty of Paris

NEW YORK

PENNSYLVANIA

NEW HAMPSHIRE
MASSACHUSETTS
RHODE ISLAND
CONNECTICUT
NEW JERSEY
DELAWARE
MARYLAND

VIRGINIA

NORTH CAROLINA

SOUTH CAROLINA

GEORGIA

Spanish Louisiana

New Orleans

Spanish Florida

Atlantic Ocean

N
W E
S

Gulf of Mexico

0   250 miles
0   400 kilometers

A treaty in 1783 with the British allowed the United States to expand.

This picture was painted at the end of Washington's second term as president.

Washington decided not to run for a third term as president. Many people wanted Washington to be president for as long as he lived. He thought two terms were enough. Because he believed in serving just two terms, the presidents after him never served more than two either, until President Franklin Roosevelt served for four terms in the 1930s and 1940s.

White House

Washington was the only president who never lived in the White House. However, he did get James Hoban to plan the White House, which took ten years to build.

Back to Mount Vernon

Washington went home to Mount Vernon in March 1797. The government's leaders thought the nation might be going to war

Six-Star General

In 1976, the United States government made Washington a six-star general. That made him the highest-ranking soldier in the history of the United States.

against France in 1798. They wanted Washington to lead the U.S. army, so he went to Philadelphia. Neither France nor the U.S. really wanted to fight, so Washington went home again.

In December 1799, Washington rode a horse around Mount Vernon on an icy day. He later

caught a cold. Doctors made him rinse out his throat with molasses, vinegar, and butter. They also put medicine made from dried beetles on his throat.

This unfinished painting of Washington was used as the model for the picture of him seen on the U.S. dollar bill.

The treatment didn't work and George Washington died on December 14, 1799. One of his generals, Henry "Lighthorse Harry" Lee, said that Washington was "first in war, first in peace, and first in the hearts of his countrymen."

Every president who came after Washington tried to do as good of a job as he did. Matching the greatness of the nation's first president will always be a worthy goal.

Washington is one of four presidents featured in a sculpture on Mount Rushmore in South Dakota.

Glossary

acre area of land about the same size as a soccer field

colony group of people who move to another land but are still ruled by the same country they moved away from. People who live in a colony are called colonists.

Constitutional Convention group of men who created a new government for the United States

Continental Congress group of men that, from 1774 to 1787, spoke and acted for the colonies that became the United States. It was formed to deal with complaints against Great Britain.

devourer someone who eats something quickly

militia group of soldiers called to fight in an emergency

mission specific type of job

plantation large farm on which one main crop is grown by workers who live there

Revolutionary War war from 1775 to 1783 in which the American colonists won freedom from Great Britain

riot fight that gets out of control

slave person who is owned by another person

surveyor person who measures and makes maps of land

term length of time an elected official serves. The term of office for the president is four years.

thresh to beat out grain from straw

tutor teacher who teaches one student at a time

widow woman whose husband has died

More Books to Read

Mello, Tara Baukus. *George Washington: First U.S. President.* Broomall, Pa.: Chelsea House Publishers, 1999.

Schaefer, Lola M. *The Washington Monument.* Chicago: Heinemann Library, 2001.

Usel, T. M. *George Washington.* Mankato, Minn.: Capstone Press, 1998.

Places to Visit

Mount Vernon Estate and Gardens

George Washington Parkway
Mount Vernon, Virginia 22121
Visitor Information: (703) 780-2000

Washington Monument

National Mall
Washington, D.C. 20024
Visitor Information: (202) 426-6841

Mount Rushmore National Memorial

Highway 244
Keystone, South Dakota 57751
Visitor Information: (605) 574-2523

Index